Sarah and Abraham

The Wonderful Promise

Told by Carine Mackenzie
Illustrations by Fred Apps

Published by Christian Focus Publications
Geanies House, Tain, Ross-shire, IV20 1TW, Scotland
Copyright © 1996 Carine Mackenzie. Reprinted 2001 and 2004
Printed in China

Sarah was a very beautiful woman. She was married to Abraham who owned lots of sheep and cattle, donkeys and camels. They had many servants working for them. But Abraham and Sarah had no children.

Abraham and Sarah lived in the city called Ur in the land of Mesopotamia.

One day God spoke to Abraham. 'Leave your home country and go to another land. I will show you where to go.'

God made a special promise to Abraham. 'I will make your family into a great nation. I will bless you. All the peoples in the world will be blessed through you.'

Sarah and Abraham and other members of the family set out on the long journey.

After they had travelled north for more than 500 miles they decided to stop in the town of Haran for a while.

God wanted them to move on so Abraham obeyed. This meant more travelling – this time southwards through the land of Canaan.

God spoke again to Sarah's husband Abraham.

'I will give this land to your children,' he said.

What a wonderful promise! Sarah had no children yet, and she was getting old.

Abraham built an altar and worshipped the Lord God. They then travelled on towards the desert accompanied by their nephew Lot.

Abraham had become even more wealthy,
owning lots of animals and gold and silver. His
nephew, Lot, also had many sheep and cattle and
tents and servants.

Life became difficult. There were so many animals belonging to Abraham and Lot that they could not find enough grass to feed them all. Soon their herdsmen began to quarrel. It was most unpleasant.

Abraham wisely decided to solve the problem.
'Let's part company,' he said to Lot. 'You choose
which way you want to go and I will go the other
way. There is plenty of land for both of us.'
So Lot chose the fruitful plains of Jordan to the
east near the wicked city of Sodom. Abraham and
Sarah went in the other direction.

God spoke to Abraham. 'Look all round this land. Your children will possess it. They will be so numerous, it will be as hard to count them as it is to count the grains of dust on the ground.' Abraham again worshipped God.

Sarah and Abraham were getting old, but they still had no son. Abraham still believed God's promise.

Sarah became impatient. She was 75 years old and Abraham 85 years. She thought she would solve the problem in her own way. She could not have a child but perhaps her maidservant would have a son for her.

She told Abraham to take Hagar her Egyptian
servant to be his wife. This created big problems in
the household. Sarah was so jealous of Hagar that
her servant had to run away. God spoke to Hagar
in the desert and told her to obey Sarah. She returned
and soon gave birth to a son named Ishmael.

Ishmael was not the son that God had promised to Abraham. He spoke again to Abraham and told him plainly that Sarah would have a son. Abraham had to laugh. He could hardly believe it.

'I will bless Ishmael,' said God. 'He will be the head of a great nation too. But Sarah's son will be the one that I have a special interest in.'

One day Abraham was sitting at the door of his tent during the hottest part of the day. He looked up and saw three men close by.

Abraham hurried over to meet them and welcomed them to his tent. 'Come and rest. Let me wash the dust from your feet. Let me get you something to eat.'

These were no ordinary visitors. The Lord had come with a message.

Abraham rushed into the tent to Sarah. 'Quick,
Sarah,' he said, 'get some flour and bake some bread
for our visitors.'

Some meat was cooked as well, and soon a fine
meal was set before the three visitors.
'Where is your wife Sarah?' they asked Abraham.
'Over there in the tent,' he replied.
'About this time next year, Sarah will have a son,'
was the Lord's message.
Sarah was listening out of sight. When she heard
these words, she laughed to herself.

How could that be possible when she and Abraham were both so old?

'Why did Sarah laugh and doubt my words?' the Lord said to Abraham. 'Is anything too hard for the Lord? Sarah will have a son.'

Sarah was afraid. She lied, 'I did not laugh,' But the Lord cannot be deceived. 'You did laugh,' he said.

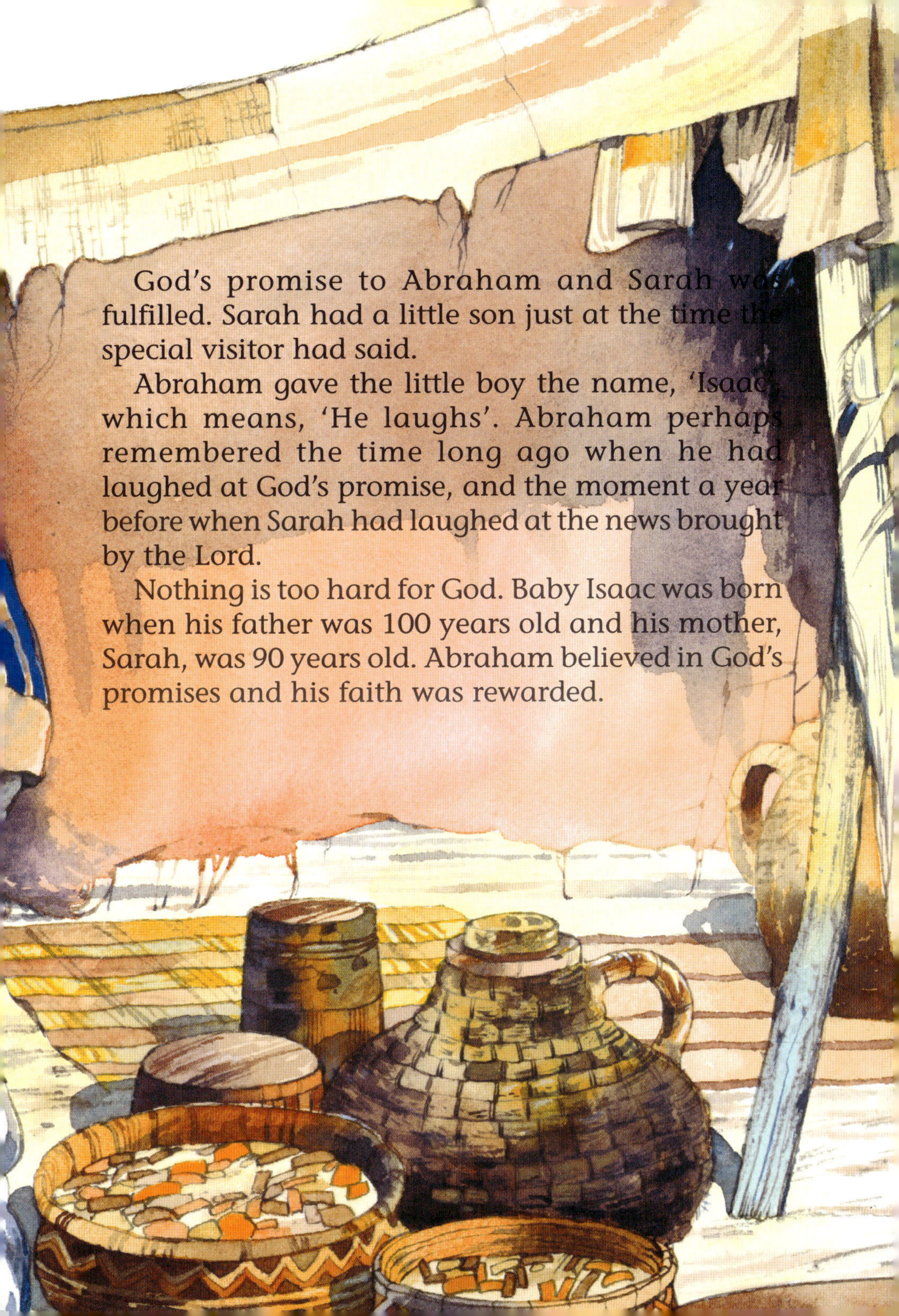

God's promise to Abraham and Sarah was fulfilled. Sarah had a little son just at the time the special visitor had said.

Abraham gave the little boy the name, 'Isaac', which means, 'He laughs'. Abraham perhaps remembered the time long ago when he had laughed at God's promise, and the moment a year before when Sarah had laughed at the news brought by the Lord.

Nothing is too hard for God. Baby Isaac was born when his father was 100 years old and his mother, Sarah, was 90 years old. Abraham believed in God's promises and his faith was rewarded.

Isaac grew up strong and healthy. When he became big enough to eat adult food, Abraham held a big party for him.

Sarah's enjoyment of the great day was spoiled. She saw Ishmael, who was now a teenager, making fun of young Isaac. Sarah was jealous.

'Get rid of that slave woman and her son,' she said to Abraham. 'That boy will never share the inheritance with Isaac.'
Abraham was upset about Sarah's outburst but God told him to do as she had said.

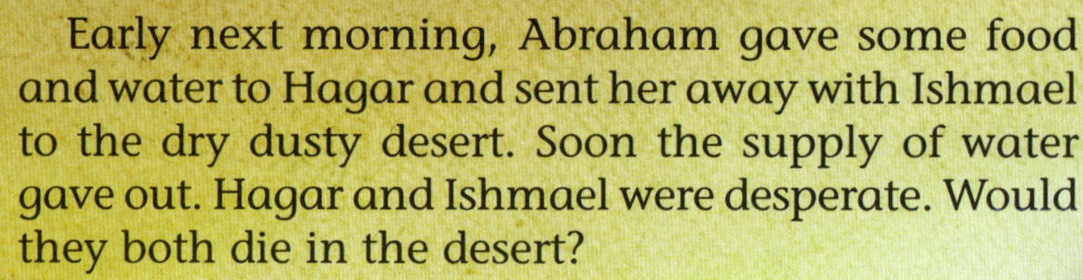

Early next morning, Abraham gave some food and water to Hagar and sent her away with Ishmael to the dry dusty desert. Soon the supply of water gave out. Hagar and Ishmael were desperate. Would they both die in the desert?

No. God heard their crying and had pity on them. Hagar noticed a well of water not far away, and their lives were saved.

God was with Ishmael as he grew up. His descendents became a strong nation as God had promised.

Isaac was Abraham and Sarah's only son. God had promised to bless their family. God tested Abraham's faith in a remarkable way.

One day God said to Abraham, 'Take Isaac, whom you love, to Mount Moriah. There, you will sacrifice him as an offering.'

Abraham believed in God. All things were possible with him. He obeyed God faithfully.

Early next morning, Abraham saddled the donkey and cut a large bundle of wood. He travelled to Mount Moriah with Isaac and two servants.

As they climbed the hill together, Isaac was puzzled.

'We have the fire and the wood here,' he said, 'but where will we get a lamb for the offering?'

'God will provide the lamb,' Abraham replied.

So the father and son continued up the mountain. When they came to the right place, Abraham built an altar and arranged the firewood on it. He tied Isaac's hands and feet and laid him on top of the wood.

Abraham believed God was in charge. He raised up the knife ready to kill Isaac. The angel of the Lord called out to him, 'Abraham, Abraham.'

'Here I am,' he replied.

'Do not harm the boy,' the angel said. 'I know that you fear God because you were willing to sacrifice your only son, Isaac.'

Then Abraham looked up and he saw a ram caught by its horns in a bush. This animal was used as the sacrifice for a burnt offering. God had indeed provided the lamb for the sacrifice.

An angel spoke to Abraham yet again, telling him that God would bless him and his family.

How glad Abraham and Isaac would have been
as they returned home to Sarah. What a welcome
she would have given them!

Sarah and Abraham had a very full and adventurous life. They had travelled many hundreds of miles. In spite of their sins and failings, God had blessed them.

God is still the same God today. With him all things are possible. He is still blessing his people in spite of their sins and wrongdoings. His greatest blessing was in sending his only Son the Lord Jesus Christ as the sacrifice for our sin.

'God demonstrates his own love for us in this: While we were still sinners, Christ died for us.' Romans 5:8